Brought to you from your friends at:

© 2012 by Jellyfish One, LLC
First Edition: Oct. 2012
Published by: Jellyfish One, LLC

Scripture references used by permission from Crossway Publishing — 2012
English Standard Version

For more information on the ESV translation please visit: www.crossway.org
Translation used by Phil Vischer in *Buck Denver Asks*™…*What's In the Bible?* DVD series.

Written and created by:
Phil Vischer, Denise George, Susan Manes & Melanie B. Rainer
Art Direction: Paul Conrad
Designed by:
Oed Ronne — Ronneland
and John Trauscht — SpringSprang Studio

BUCK DENVER & FRIENDS™ PRESENT...

EVERYDAY EMMANUEL

MAKING THE MOST OF CHRISTMAS FOR BUSY FAMILIES

TABLE OF CONTENTS

Introduction 4

Part 1: Countdown to Christmas Calendar 7

Part 2: What is Advent? 19

Part 3: Big Questions about Christmas 25

Part 4: Weekly Advent & Big Question Activities 27

Part 5: Calendar Activities (Activity "Cut-Outs") 57

Part 6: Provided Printable Activities 73

INTRODUCTION

Christmastime often becomes busy-time. It is so easy for the "to-do" lists, errands and events this time of year to unintentionally overshadow meaningful family time and what you and your family truly hold important this time of year. This year, celebrate *Everyday Emmanuel* by thoughtfully spending time together as a family.

What is Everyday Emmanuel? It's a fun, easy-to-use family Christmas Countdown experience designed to help families make the most of Christmas and better understand the true meaning of the season. Our prayer is that *Everyday Emmanuel* will allow your family to spend intentional time together celebrating old and new traditions. *Everyday Emmanuel* makes it easy for your family to explore the meaning of Advent and offers you the opportunity to add a deeper spiritual meaning to the season by understanding how many of today's traditions point directly back to Jesus – that indeed God is With Us (Emmanuel) everyday!

Isn't that truly Good News?

The memories you make with your children will last longer than any gift you place under the tree.

What's included:

- Instructions to Make & Use Your Countdown to Christmas Calendar
- Weekly Advent Devotionals & Ornament Activity
- Weekly Big Questions About Christmas & Discussion Guide
- Family Activity List (broken down by time required and easy to use to fill in your calendar)
- Seven "print and use" activities
- Online access to videos & additional resources
- Helpful tips throughout the book to save you time & money

Calendar:

Your calendar will provide the framework for *Everyday Emmanuel* and serve as a fun visual for your family to anticipate Christmas day together. **Kick off the fun by making your own calendar together before December 1.** Then use the calendar to count each day leading up to Christmas in a meaningful way. You can use all the resources we provide for an easy guide or add in your own traditions as you see fit.

Advent Devotionals & Activities:

Each Sunday of Advent has a specific purpose, to remember the suffering of the Israelites through the Old Testament and to prepare for the coming King Jesus. Each Sunday is celebrated with the lighting of that week's candle on an Advent wreath. We've provided a devotional your family can do together for each Sunday of Advent.

Each advent devotional includes a corresponding ornament you can make for your tree. You may decide to create your ornament at the same time as the devotional or use the ornament as an additional activity for your family that week.

Big Questions About Christmas:

The Big Questions About Christmas are designed to help your family explore the tensions between the Christmas they see in stores and on television, and the Christmas they hear about in church. Each week, we've provided a brief family discussion guide including a video, discussion questions, and prayer time for your family.

Family Time Activities:

Meaningful family time doesn't have to take hours to plan or a lot of money. We've provided a variety of suggestions to help jump-start your time together as a family this December. Some activities only take a few minutes while others may take longer. Pick and choose what works best for you on any give day. We've broken our ideas up by the amount of time each activity takes to make it easier for you. We've also included space to write in your own traditions & ideas.

Online Access:

To access the Big Questions About Christmas videos, to print off additional activity pages, and more visit: **www.whatsinthebible.com/everydayemmanuel**

Your password is: **advent**

Part 1:

THE COUNTDOWN TO CHRISTMAS CALENDAR

Your Guide to Making Your Own Countdown to Christmas Calendar

The purpose of making your own Countdown to Christmas Calendar is to:

- Give your children a visual way to anticipate spending time together each day as they wait for Christmas Day

- Easily count down how many days remain until Christmas Day

- Provide the framework to celebrate the traditional Sundays of Advent and watch our Big Questions About Christmas each week

How It Works:

1. Create your own calendar on or before December 1. We've provided instructions below.

2. The calendar will start out with 25 empty pockets, which you will make from letter-sized envelopes.

3. Starting on December 1, you will fill that day's pocket with a note that states what activity the family will do together that day. (We've provided pages of cut-out activity ideas to help you get started.)

4. Each day have the kids take turns announcing to the family what the note says the day's activity will be.

 TIP! Have older kids help those who can't read yet or draw pictures for the days it's your younger child's turn.

5. Spend time together completing the day's activity.

 TIP! Don't forget to use your Advent activities for Sundays and your Big Questions About Christmas on Thursdays (or another day of the week).

6. As you complete each day, keep the note in that day's space. You'll then be able to see a reminder of how you've spent time together this Christmas season with each completed space, and how many days remain until Christmas Day with each empty space.

7. Repeat each day until you get to Christmas Day!

Remember, it's about making memories, not adding stress to your day!

- Don't get overwhelmed with needing a big activity each day. We've provided lots of ideas with different levels of time commitment and space to write in your own.

- It's okay to have an empty spot on your calendar--everyone's busy. If you run out of time some days, consider letting your children write their favorite moment from the day and putting it in that day's space to mark that day.

- Repeat your favorite activities throughout the month.

Here's an example of what your activities you could look like the first few days:

Dec. 1	Dec. 2	Dec. 3	Dec. 4	Dec. 5
Each person gets to pick a favorite Christmas song to listen to today in the car.	Today we'll light our first Advent candle & read about its meaning.	Busy day--have the kids write their favorite moment of the day down.	Play a favorite board game together.	Pop some popcorn and watch a Big Question About Christmas video.

Part 1: Countdown to Christmas Calendar

How to Make Your Own Calendar:

Kick off your family time by making your own Countdown to Christmas Calendar!

Supplies Needed:

- 13-16 envelopes (we recommend white, 3 5/8" x 6 ½")
- Large poster board
- A thick sharpie or black marker
- Glue or tape
- Decorating supplies (optional decorations included)
- Scissors

 TIP! Visit whatsinthebible.com/everydayemmanuel and enter the password "advent" for links to purchase all the supplies you need online.

Step 1: Seal 13 envelopes (with nothing inside). Then cut each envelope in half. You will have 26 pockets for your calendar after this step. (You'll have one extra in case you need a do-over.)

Step 2: Give each pocket a number starting with 1 and ending at 25. Make sure the opening of the pocket is at the top when you write your numbers and write on the smooth side.

Step 3: What about decorations? When to decorate your poster board and pockets is completely up to you. You may want to decorate each pocket before you assemble the calendar or you may want to see how the layout looks and then decorate. You decide! We recommend at least highlighting your Advent Sundays with a special symbol or picture. We've shown this using a candle on days 2, 9, 16, and 23, in our example for 2012.

Step 4: Glue the pockets to your poster board starting with 1 and ending with 25. We recommend laying all the pockets out before you start gluing so you can make sure they all fit.

Step 5: Hang the calendar somewhere everyone can see it, like the fridge, door, or hallway.

The cut-out activity sheets to use with your calendar are included in Part 5 of your *Everyday Emmanuel* book.

Countdown to Christmas Calendar – Decorations

Cut out these fun decorations to use for your Countdown to Christmas Calendar! If you'd rather not cut your calendar decorations out of your book, visit **www.whatsinthebible.com/everydayemmanuel** and enter the password **"advent"** to access printable versions.

Banner for Top of Calendar

COUNTDOWN TO CHRISTMAS

Part 1: Countdown to Christmas Calendar

TIP! This page is INTENTIONALLY LEFT BLANK for those who choose to use the cut-outs from the book rather than printing. Remember, if you'd like to print the cut-outs, you can visit **www.whatsinthebible.com/everydayemmanuel** and enter the password "**advent**" to access printable versions.

Character Cut-Outs

Part 1: Countdown to Christmas Calendar

TIP! This page is INTENTIONALLY LEFT BLANK for those who choose to use the cut-outs from the book rather than printing. Remember, if you'd like to print the cut-outs, you can visit **www.whatsinthebible.com/everydayemmanuel** and enter the password "**advent**" to access printable versions.

Advent Candle Cut-Outs

Part 1: Countdown to Christmas Calendar

TIP! This page is INTENTIONALLY LEFT BLANK for those who choose to use the cut-outs from the book rather than printing. Remember, if you'd like to print the cut-outs, you can visit **www.whatsinthebible.com/everydayemmanuel** and enter the password "**advent**" to access printable versions.

Part 2:
WHAT IS ADVENT?

What is Advent?

Read this Advent poem as a family, then watch the "What is Advent?" video at **whatsinthebible.com/everydayemmanuel**, using the password **"advent"**. Then make an advent wreath together!

TIP! This can be one of your first week activities on your Countdown to Christmas Calendar, or you can do it on the first Sunday of Advent before your Advent Devotional.

An Advent Poem

Four weeks in December – Filled with good cheer!
As churches remember that Christmas is near!
A time we call Advent whose purpose is clear
To count down the weeks until Jesus is here!

The Israelites waited
For hundreds of years
To welcome the one
Who could conquer their fears

And pay for their sins
And save them from death
They watched and they waited
They all held their breath

So once every week
A candle we light
To celebrate Jesus
And chase out the night

A Savior! Messiah!
A conquering king!
The four weeks of Advent can be just the thing

To focus our hearts
As Christmas draws near – Hurray! Hallelujah!
Our savior is here!

How To Make An Advent Wreath (Optional)

There are many different ways your family can make an Advent wreath! You can purchase one pre-made online, or you can make your own. You may also be seeing an Advent wreath lit at your church, and can use these devotionals at home to discuss it with your family.

 TIP! Visit whatsinthebible.com/everydayemmanuel using the password "advent" for links to all of the supplies you need.

Elements of the Advent Wreath:

- Evergreen Wreath
- 3 purple candles
- 1 pink candle
- 1 white candle

To build your Advent wreath, here are some suggestions:

1. You can purchase a pre-made Advent wreath frame, which you may place inside of an evergreen wreath. These frames hold 5 tall taper candles.

2. You can make your own wreath frame, or not use a frame at all. Substitutions include buying candles in small glass jars and setting them inside of your evergreen wreath.

3. If you don't have space for a wreath, or want to display your Advent candles, you can decorate a mantle or table with evergreen boughs and place the candles (in containers or on a glass plate) along the surface.

Symbolism in the Advent Wreath:

Evergreen wreath: The evergreen symbolizes the never-failing love of Christ, similar to the tradition of the Christmas tree.

Colored Candles: Traditionally, Advent wreaths are made with 3 purple candles to emphasize that Advent is a season of repentance. Some traditions include fasting as a part of Advent, and purple is associated with periods of fasting. Purple is also the color of royalty, representing Christ the King. The third week has a pink candle to mark the beginning of the celebration of Christ's birth.

4 Candles: Some believe the 4 candles celebrate the 400-year intertestamental period between the end of the Old Testament and the coming of Christ. The light the candles provide each week symbolizes that Jesus is the light of the world.

Advent Weekly Overview

Each week of Advent has a specific purpose, to remember the suffering of the Israelites and to prepare for the coming King. Each week is celebrated with the lighting of that week's candle on the Advent Wreath. Advent is designed to be a time of reflection and anticipation, leading up to the birth of Christ on Christmas. The traditional Church calendar allows for 12 days of Christmas, from December 25 to

January 6 (which marks the day the Magi visited the Christ child). This celebration is called Epiphany.

There are many different sequences you can follow for the Advent candles. Some traditions follow "prophecy, annunciation, proclamation, fulfillment" and some use the framework of people with "Isaiah, John the Baptist, Mary, the Magi". We've chosen to use the tradition of the words "Hope, Peace, Joy, Love" to lead your family through this Advent season.

- **First Week of Advent:** Candle of Hope
  This week, we encourage your family to read some of the Old Testament prophecies about the Messiah, remembering how the Israelites longed for a king.

- **Second Week of Advent:** Candle of Peace
  Isaiah called Jesus the "prince of peace". This week, we encourage your family to read about the peace Jesus brings to the world and to our hearts.

- **Third Week of Advent:** Candle of Joy
  This week, we encourage you to celebrate the birth of Christ and read Mary's Magnificat to remember how overjoyed the people were that their King had come.

- **Fourth Week of Advent:** Candle of Love
  The final week of Advent is set aside to praise God for His great love – love so strong that it would cause Him to send His only son to die for our sins.

TIP! We hope this time with your family becomes something very special during this busy Advent season. Feel free to use this as a starting point for family time, or use it word for word. Only you know what is best for your family! We encourage you to rotate these activities among your family – let one child read the scripture, another one open or close in prayer, etc.

Part 3:

What are the Big Questions About Christmas?

The Big Questions About Christmas are designed to help your family explore the tensions between the Christmas they see in stores and on television, and the Christmas they hear about in church. Each week, we've provided a short family guide including a video, discussion questions, and prayer time for your family.

How to Access the Online Videos

To access the exclusive videos from *Why Do We Call It Christmas?* for *Everyday Emmanuel*, go to: **www.whatsinthebible.com/everydayemmanuel**

Enter the password: **advent**

Follow the instructions on screen and in the discussion guide to find the video for each week.

Weekly Overview

- **Week 1: Why do we call it Christmas?**
  Starting at the very beginning – why do we even call Christmas "Christmas"? Your family will learn the history of the word Christmas and celebrate the truth at the root of the word – Christ!

- **Week 2: What do Christmas trees have to do with Jesus?**
  This week, your family will learn the history of the Christmas tree and how these beloved decorations point back to Jesus.

- **Week 3: Who is Santa Claus?**
  No spoilers – we promise! But mom or dad may want to watch this video before you watch it as a family. This week, learn about Saint Nicholas, a church bishop from the 300s and how he became a part of our Christmas traditions.

- **Week 4: Bonus Videos: Who is Emmanuel? And Luke 2**
  Watch these bonus videos during the 4th week of Advent to learn more about Emmanuel – God with us!

Part 4:
WEEKLY ADVENT DEVOTIONALS & BIG QUESTIONS ABOUT CHRISTMAS FAMILY GUIDES

FIRST WEEK OF ADVENT

1. Candle of Hope Devotional for First Sunday of Advent

2. HOPE Ornament

3. Big Question About Christmas: Why Do We Call It Christmas?

 TIP! Don't forget to fill in your Countdown to Christmas Calendar with family activities for this week! Ideas for the remaining days can be found in Part 5.

First Week of Advent: The Candle of Hope

This week, we are starting our celebration of Advent by lighting the first candle in our Advent wreath – the Candle of Hope.

PRAY

What were some of your favorite things that happened today? Let's pray to God and thank Him for those things! We can also ask Him to bless our time together as a family.

TALK

Tonight we are going to light the first candle on our Advent wreath – the Candle of Hope! How would you describe hope? What are some things you hope for?

The Israelites waited for many years for the Messiah that the prophets had promised. Their kingdom of Israel had been conquered and other people had tried to kill the Israelites. God sent prophets to remind them that He would take care of them. How do you think the Israelites felt waiting for so many years for the Messiah to come?

READ

Let's read some of God's word together.

- **Isaiah 7:14**
- **Isaiah 9:6**
- **Micah 5:2**
- **Revelation 21:1-7**

TALK

In that last passage, we are promised that Jesus will come again one day. Jesus promised that He would one day return again to us and that all things would be made new in Christ. There will be no more tears or suffering. In this season of Advent, we celebrate that Jesus came once, but also prepare ourselves for Him to come again!

SING

Let's sing a song together to worship the Lord. **O Come, O Come Emmanuel** is one of the most beautiful songs we can sing at Advent. As we sing it together, let's think about how the Israelites must have felt waiting for the Messiah to come.

O come, O Come Emmanuel
And ransom captive Israel,
That mourns in lonely exile here
Until the Son of God appear.

Rejoice! Rejoice! Emmanuel
Shall come to thee, O Israel.

O come Thou Rod of Jesse, free
Thine own from Satan's tyranny;
From depths of hell Thy people save,
And give them victory o'er the grave.

Rejoice! Rejoice! Emmanuel
Shall come to thee, O Israel.

O come Thou Day-Spring,
come and cheer
Our spirits by Thine advent here;
Disperse the gloomy clouds of night
And death's dark shadows put to flight!

Rejoice! Rejoice! Emmanuel
Shall come to thee, O Israel.

Rejoice! Rejoice! Emmanuel
Shall come to thee, O Israel.

— Public Domain

LIGHT THE CANDLE

Light the first purple candle on your advent wreath and say this prayer:

Thank You, Father God, for Your many blessings, for sending Your Son Jesus Christ, the Messiah, to the people of Israel and to us. Thank You for the promise of Hope – hope for the Israelites, and hope for us today. Amen.

 TIP! Create your HOPE ornament as one of your family activities this week.

HOPE Ornament

Materials Needed:

- HOPE Ornament cut-out
- Scissors
- Hole Punch
- Ribbon or Yarn
- Decorating items, such as glue and glitter, crayons, etc.

 TIP! Tape or glue your ornament to an extra piece of poster board or card stock and then cut it out to help the ornament hang better on the tree.

Instructions:

Cut out the HOPE ornament below. Decorate it however you want – with crayons, markers, or use glue and different colors of glitter for each letter. Punch out the hole, tie a piece of ribbon or yarn through it, and hang it on your Christmas tree!

 TIP! You can print extra copies of the HOPE Ornament at **whatsinthebible.com/everydayemmanuel** using the password "**advent**". You'll also find easy cut-outs for all of the ornaments on pages 45 & 46.

Big Questions About Christmas Week 1:
Why do we call it Christmas?

TALK

Tonight we're going to find out why Christmas is called Christmas! What are your favorite parts of Christmastime?

Does anybody have any idea why Christmas is called Christmas? Here's a hint! Who do we celebrate at Christmas?

WATCH

Visit **www.whatsinthebible.com/everydayemmanuel**. Enter the password **"advent"**. Click on "Big Questions About Christmas". Then click on the link for **"Week 1: Why do we call it Christmas?"** and watch the video.

DISCUSS

What did you think of the video? Do you remember the two words that make up the word "Christmas"?

Christmas helps us remember the whole life of Christ – His coming to earth as a tiny baby, and the reason why He came – to die so that we can be with Him forever. What are some ways we can remember Christ as a family this Christmas?

Let's make a list of some of those ways!

_____

_____

_____

_____

_____

PRAY

Pray together as a family.

First Week Activity Cut-Outs

If you want to make these activities part of your Countdown to Christmas Calendar, cut out these slips of paper and put them into the pockets for the days you want to do them. We also provide many more activities at the end of Everyday Emmanuel that you can use to fill in the other days this week.

Visit **www.whatsinthebible.com/everydayemmanuel** and enter the password "**advent**." Then click on "**Activities**" to access a printable version of this page.

First Sunday of Advent: Read the family devotional and light the Candle of Hope

---

Big Question: Why do we call it Christmas?

Make your HOPE Ornament

SECOND WEEK OF ADVENT

1. Candle of Peace Devotional for the Second Sunday of Advent

2. PEACE Ornament

3. Big Question About Christmas: Why do we have Christmas trees?

 TIP! Don't forget to fill in your Countdown to Christmas Calendar with family activities for this week! Ideas for the remaining days can be found in Part 5.

Second Week of Advent: The Candle of Peace

This week, we will light two candles on our Advent wreath – we will re-light the Candle of Hope from last week, and add the Candle of Peace.

PRAY

What were some of your favorite things that happened this week? Isn't it amazing how much God blesses us? Let's pray together as a family, praising God for those good things and asking Him to bless our time together.

TALK

When you think of "peace," what comes to mind? There are many different kinds of peace – world peace, peace between enemies, and peace in our hearts. Can you think of places in the world where there isn't peace today?

We read last week in Isaiah that Jesus is called the "Prince of Peace". What do you think that means?

READ

Let's read some of God's messages about peace from the Bible.

- **Isaiah 54:10**
- **John 14:27**
- **Philippians 4:6-7**

TALK

Jesus came to bring peace to everything! He is the Prince of Peace! He promises us peace in our hearts – a peace that goes beyond the things that make us upset everyday. Are there times when you feel frustrated or afraid? Do you want to share some of those moments with us?

In those moments, you can pray to God and ask Him to give you peace and patience. He also promises that one day, when Jesus comes again, there will be no more suffering – finally, there will be peace throughout the whole world!

SING

Let's sing a song together that can remind us of the peace that God brings – *Silent Night* is about the night Jesus was born, the night when Peace came to Earth!

Silent Night, Holy Night
All is calm, all is bright
Round yon virgin, mother and child
Holy infant so tender and mild
Sleep in heavenly peace
Sleep in heavenly peace

Silent Night, Holy Night
Shepherds quake at the sight
Glories stream from heaven afar
Heavenly hosts sing Alleluia!
Christ the Savior is born
Christ the Savior is born

Silent Night, Holy Night
Son of God, love's pure light
Radiant beams from Thy holy face
With the dawn of redeeming grace
Jesus, Lord at Thy birth
Jesus, Lord at Thy birth

— Public Domain

LIGHT THE CANDLE

Light the first candle on your advent wreath – the Candle of Hope.

Then, light the second purple candle on your advent wreath – the Candle of Peace, and say this prayer:

Father God, tonight we pray and thank You for your wonderful gift of peace. We pray for peace in the many areas of the world tonight where there isn't peace, where there is war and suffering. We also pray for peace in our hearts during this very busy season. In Christ's name, Amen.

TIP! Create your PEACE Ornament as one of your family activities this week.

PEACE Ornament

Materials Needed:

- PEACE Ornament cut-out
- Scissors
- Hole Punch
- Ribbon or Yarn
- Decorating items, such as glue and glitter, crayons, etc.

 TIP! Tape or glue your ornament to an extra piece of poster board or card stock and then cut it out to help the ornament hang better on the tree.

Instructions:

Cut out the PEACE ornament below. Decorate it however you want – with crayons, markers, or use glue and different colors of glitter for each letter. Punch out the hole, tie a piece of ribbon or yarn through it, and hang it on your Christmas tree!

 TIP! You can print extra copies of the PEACE Ornament at **whatsinthebible.com/everydayemmanuel** using the password "**advent**". You'll also find easy cut-outs for all of the ornaments on pages 45 & 46.

Big Questions About Christmas Week 2:
Why do we have Christmas trees?

WATCH

Visit **www.whatsinthebible.com/everydayemmanuel**. Enter the password **"advent"**. Click on "Big Questions About Christmas". Then click on the link for **"Week 2: Why do we have Christmas trees?"** Watch the video!

DISCUSS

Wow! What a crazy story. St. Boniface was a really brave man. Why do you think he stood up to the worshipers of Thor?

Christmas is a wonderful time to share the love of Jesus with the people in our lives, like St. Boniface did! Are there people in our life with whom we could share the true meaning of Christmas? What are some different ways we can use our actions to show the love of Jesus to other people this Christmas?

Let's make a list of some of them!

_____
_____
_____
_____
_____
_____

PRAY

Pray together as a family.

Second Week Activity Cut-Outs

If you want to make these activities part of your Countdown to Christmas Calendar, cut out these slips of paper and put them into the pockets for the days you want to do them. We also provide many more activities at the end of Everyday Emmanuel that you can use to fill in the other days this week.

Visit **www.whatsinthebible.com/everydayemmanuel** and enter the password "**advent**." Then click on "**Activities**" to access a printable version of this page.

Second Sunday of Advent: Read the family devotional and light the Candle of Peace

---

Big Question: Why do we have Christmas trees?

Make your PEACE Ornament

THIRD WEEK OF ADVENT

1. Candle of Joy Devotional for the Third Sunday of Advent

2. JOY Ornament

3. Big Question About Christmas: Who is Santa Claus?

 TIP! Don't forget to fill in your Countdown to Christmas Calendar with family activities for this week! Ideas for the remaining days can be found in Part 5.

Part 4: Weekly Advent Devotionals & Big Questions About Christmas Family Guides

Third Week of Advent: The Candle of Joy

This week, we get to light 3 candles on our Advent wreath! Do you remember what the first 2 candles represent?

First, we will re-light the Candles of Hope and Peace. This week, we'll add the Candle of Joy!

PRAY

What are some events or people that brought you joy this week? Let's pray thanking God for each one of them!

TALK

This week we're lighting the Candle of Joy! Why do you think joy might be an important thing to have this time of year?

The last two weeks, we've been lighting candles that remind us of difficult things – the suffering of the Israelites and the lack of peace in the world. We can be grateful that Jesus came to Earth to end our suffering and to bring peace. And we can celebrate it too!

READ

Let's read some verses from the Bible that remind us to celebrate Jesus!

- Luke 2: 8-14
- Luke 1:46-55 (Mary's Magnificat)
- 1 Peter 1:8-9
- Isaiah 12: 5-6

TALK

Christmas is such a fun time of year – especially when we understand why Jesus came to Earth. How does it make you feel to know that Jesus was born for you – and for everyone else – so that we can be with Him forever, in a world without suffering?

What are some ways we can celebrate Jesus this Christmas? What are some ways we can share our joy with the people in our lives? Let's brainstorm together as a family how we can share the joy of Jesus this Christmas!

SING

What song do you think would be fun to sing to celebrate Jesus? How about *Joy to the World*?

Joy to the world
The Lord has come
Let earth receive her King
Let every heart prepare Him room
And Heaven and nature sing,
And Heaven and nature sing
And Heaven and Heaven and nature sing!

He rules the world with truth and grace,
And makes the nations prove
The glories of His righteousness
And wonders of His love
And wonders of His love
And wonders, wonders, of His love!

— Public Domain

LIGHT THE CANDLES

Let's light the first two Advent candles on our wreath – the purple ones for hope and peace.

Now let's light this week's candle – the pink Candle of Joy.

As we light it, let's say this prayer:

Dear God, thank you so much for sending your Son to us as a baby. We love to celebrate Christmas each year, and please help us to always remember that it is a celebration of You and Your promises that have come true. Please fill our hearts with hope, peace and joy this Christmas season. In Christ's name, Amen.

 TIP! Create your JOY Ornament as one of your family activities this week.

JOY Ornament

Materials Needed:

- JOY Ornament cut-out
- Scissors
- Hole Punch
- Ribbon or Yarn
- Decorating items, such as glue and glitter, crayons, etc.

 TIP! Tape or glue your ornament to an extra piece of poster board or card stock and then cut it out to help the ornament hang better on the tree.

Instructions:

Cut out the JOY ornament below. Decorate it however you want – with crayons, markers, or use glue and different colors of glitter for each letter. Punch out the hole, tie a piece of ribbon or yarn through it, and hang it on your Christmas tree!

 TIP! You can print extra copies of the JOY Ornament at **whatsinthebible.com/everydayemmanuel** using the password "**advent**". You'll also find easy cut-outs for all of the ornaments on pages 45 & 46.

Big Questions About Christmas Week 3:
Who is Santa Claus?

 TIP! There are **no Santa Claus spoilers** in the video, but Mom or Dad may want to watch the video ahead of time to be prepared for any questions.

 ### WATCH

Visit **www.whatsinthebible.com/everydayemmanuel**. Enter the password **"advent"**. Click on "Big Questions About Christmas". Then click on the link for **"Week 3: Who is Santa Claus?"**. Watch the video!

 ### DISCUSS

Wow! We can learn so much from Saint Nicholas – it's obvious he really loved Jesus and that's why he did so many kind things.

What are some of the ways Saint Nicholas showed the love of Jesus?

At Christmas time, we think a lot about the presents we're receiving. Let's think of some special ways as a family we can *give* this Christmas and make a list:

_____

_____

_____

_____

_____

_____

 ### PRAY

Pray as a family.

Third Week Activity Cut-Outs

If you want to make these activities part of your Countdown to Christmas Calendar, cut out these slips of paper and put them into the pockets for the days you want to do them. We also provide many more activities at the end of Everyday Emmanuel that you can use to fill in the other days this week.

Visit **www.whatsinthebible.com/everydayemmanuel** and enter the password "**advent**." Then click on "**Activities**" to access a printable version of this page.

Third Sunday of Advent: Read the family devotional and light the Candle of Joy

---

Big Question: Who is Santa Claus?

Make your JOY Ornament

FOURTH WEEK OF ADVENT

1. Candle of Love for the Fourth Sunday of Advent Devotional

2. Christ Candle for Christmas Eve or Christmas Day Devotional

3. LOVE ornament

Fourth Week of Advent: The Candle of Love

This is the last week of Advent! We will light the 4 outer candles on our wreath tonight, and then we will light the final center candle on Christmas Eve.

Do you remember what the first 3 candles represent? Hope, Peace and Joy! Tonight we will light the Candle of Love.

PRAY

Who are some of your favorite people? Let's pray to God and thank Him for sending those people into our lives. Let's also ask Him to bless those people this Christmas!

TALK

This week we are lighting the Candle of Love! Do you usually think of the word "love" when you think of Christmas? What love do you think we might be celebrating this week?

When God sent His son Jesus to earth, it was the ultimate expression of how much He loves us! Christmas is not only a time to be thankful for Jesus, but to remember just how much God loves all of us.

READ

God's Word is full of reminders of how much He loves us! Let's read some of them together.

- **Deuteronomy 7:9**
- **John 3:16**
- **1 John 4:7-11**

SING

Tonight let's sing *Hark the Herald Angels Sing!* It reminds us of all the promises that were fulfilled through Christ.

*Hark the herald angels sing
Glory to the newborn King!
Peace on earth and mercy mild
God and sinners reconciled
Joyful, all ye nations rise
Join the triumph of the skies
With the angelic host proclaim
Christ is born in Bethlehem
Hark the herald angels sing
Glory to the newborn King!*

*Hail the Heaven-born Prince of Peace
Hail the Son of Righteousness
Light and life to all He brings
Risen with healing in His wings
Mild He lays His glory by
Born that man no more may die
Born to raise the sons of earth
Born to give them second birth
Hark! The herald angels sing
Glory to the newborn King!*

— Public Domain

TALK

Think about all of the things we've learned together about Christmas during Advent! Do you remember some of the things we talked about each week?

Isn't it amazing how many of God's promises came true through Jesus? The hope of the Israelites was finally fulfilled, and we still have so much to hope for in Jesus. Jesus came to bring peace to the whole world and to our hearts. We celebrate the joy of His birth and the love God has for us during Christmas!

LIGHT THE CANDLES

Let's light the first 3 candles on our Advent wreath - the first two purple ones for hope and peace and then the pink one for joy.

Now let's light the final purple candle – the Candle of Love.

As we light it, let's say this prayer:

Dear God, thank you for loving us so much that you would send your son Jesus to earth. Thank you for the gift of His love and for all of the other gifts you have given to us. Help us to remember the real meaning of Christmas, and please fill our hearts with hope, peace, joy and love. In Christ's name, Amen.

Part 4: Weekly Advent Devotionals & Big Questions About Christmas Family Guides

Christmas Eve: The Christ Candle

This is a short devotional for Christmas Eve or Christmas Day. We know many families have their own Christmas Eve traditions, so feel free to include this in your normal celebration or just do your own thing!

It's Christmas Eve! Advent is almost over, and tonight we will light the last candle – the Christ Candle. Christ is the heart of Christmas – He is what it is all about!

READ or WATCH

Read Luke 2 together as a family, or watch a special video of Luke 2 at **whatsinthe-bible.com/everydayemmanuel** using the password **"advent"**.

LIGHT THE CANDLES

Let's light the 4 outside candles on our Advent wreath – the candles of hope, peace, joy and love.

Now let's light the final candle – the white one in the center. This is the Christ candle.

SING

Let's sing *O Little Town of Bethlehem* as we watch the candles flicker, and remember the great gift of the Baby Jesus on this night so many years ago in Bethlehem.

O little town of Bethlehem
How still we see thee lie
Above thy deep and dreamless sleep
The silent stars go by
Yet in the dark streets shineth
The everlasting Light
The hopes and fears of all the years
Are met in Thee tonight

— Public Domain

LOVE Ornament

Materials Needed:

- LOVE Ornament cut-out
- Scissors
- Hole Punch
- Ribbon or Yarn
- Decorating items, such as glue and glitter, crayons, etc.

TIP! Tape or glue your ornament to an extra piece of poster board or card stock and then cut it out to help the ornament hang better on the tree.

Instructions:

Cut out the LOVE ornament below. Decorate it however you want – with crayons, markers, or use glue and different colors of glitter for each letter. Punch out the hole, tie a piece of ribbon or yarn through it, and hang it on your Christmas tree!

TIP! You can print extra copies of the LOVE Ornament at **whatsinthebible.com/everydayemmanuel** using the password "**advent**". You'll also find easy cut-outs for all of the ornaments on pages 45 & 46.

Part 4: Weekly Advent Devotionals & Big Questions About Christmas Family Guides

Fourth Week Activity Cut-Outs

If you want to make these activities part of your Countdown to Christmas Calendar, cut out these slips of paper and put them into the pockets for the days you want to do them. We also provide many more activities at the end of Everyday Emmanuel that you can use to fill in the other days this week.

Visit **www.whatsinthebible.com/everydayemmanuel** and enter the password **"advent."** Then click on **"Activities"** to access a printable version of this page.

Fourth Sunday of Advent: Read the family devotional and light the Candle of Love

---

Read the Christmas Eve family devotional and light the Christ Candle

---

Make your LOVE Ornament

Ornament Cut-Outs

TIP! Visit **www.whatsinthebible.com/everydayemmanuel** and enter the password **"advent."** Then click on **"Advent Ornaments"** to access a printable version of this page.

Part 4: Weekly Advent Devotionals & Big Questions About Christmas Family Guides

TIP! This page is INTENTIONALLY LEFT BLANK for those who choose to use the cut-outs from the book rather than printing. Remember, if you'd like to print the cut-outs, you can visit **www.whatsinthebible.com/everydayemmanuel** and enter the password "**advent**" to access printable versions.

Ornament Cut-Outs

TIP! Visit **www.whatsinthebible.com/everydayemmanuel** and enter the password **"advent."** Then click on **"Advent Ornaments"** to access a printable version of this page.

TIP! This page is INTENTIONALLY LEFT BLANK for those who choose to use the cut-outs from the book rather than printing. Remember, if you'd like to print the cut-outs, you can visit **www.whatsinthebible.com/everydayemmanuel** and enter the password "**advent**" to access printable versions.

Part 5:

ACTIVITIES FOR THE COUNTDOWN TO CHRISTMAS CALENDAR

TIP! This page is INTENTIONALLY LEFT BLANK for those who choose to use the cut-outs from the book rather than printing. Remember, if you'd like to print the cut-outs, you can visit **www.whatsinthebible.com/everydayemmanuel** and enter the password "**advent**" to access printable versions.

TIP! Use these ideas (and cut-outs) for the remaining days in your Countdown to Christmas Calendar. Printables for several of these activities are provided in Part 6. These provided activities are marked with an asterisks (*).

To print your activity cut-outs, go to **www.whatsinthebible.com/everydayemmanuel** and enter the password "**advent**". Then click on "**Activities.**"

10 minutes

Read a Christmas book aloud.

Pick a favorite Christmas song or CD to listen to in the car today.

Give an early Christmas gift to your children.
(Ideas include a new Christmas CD or movie, Christmas socks, special treats or candy.)

Hide a special gift or note under each child's pillow or bed so they find it in the morning or before bed.

Enjoy a special Christmas treat today like candy canes.

Call a friend or relative and wish them a Merry Christmas.

TIP! This page is INTENTIONALLY LEFT BLANK for those who choose to use the cut-outs from the book rather than printing. Remember, if you'd like to print the cut-outs, you can visit **www.whatsinthebible.com/everydayemmanuel** and enter the password **"advent"** to access printable versions.

- Give your mail carrier or local delivery person a Christmas card or warm drink.

- Pay for the person's meal or drink behind you in line at the drive-thru and ask that they be wished Merry Christmas.

- Count how many Christmas cards are in the mail.

- See who in the family can pick out the best Christmas themed outfit.

- Read Luke 2 together.

- Make hot chocolate.

- Complete the What I Love About Christmas printable.*

- Send someone an Everyday Emmanuel Christmas card.*

TIP! This page is INTENTIONALLY LEFT BLANK for those who choose to use the cut-outs from the book rather than printing. Remember, if you'd like to print the cut-outs, you can visit **www.whatsinthebible.com/everydayemmanuel** and enter the password "**advent**" to access printable versions.

30 min. to 1 hour

Play Christmas BINGO. *

Take Buck Denver's Christmas Word Challenge .*

Color a Buck Denver and Friends coloring page. *

Cut-out and display your Christmas verse cut-outs & color the matching coloring pages.*

Wrap Christmas presents together.

Go on a family drive to look at Christmas lights in the area.

Play a favorite board game together.

Make root beer floats for a special treat.

TIP! This page is INTENTIONALLY LEFT BLANK for those who choose to use the cut-outs from the book rather than printing. Remember, if you'd like to print the cut-outs, you can visit **www.whatsinthebible.com/everydayemmanuel** and enter the password "**advent**" to access printable versions.

Ask your kids to create a special "Christmas program" and perform it for you. This is a great chance to showcase any music or dance pieces they've been working on.

Take Christmas cookies to a neighbor or person in need.

Spend time looking at family pictures from past holidays and celebrations together and let each person pick a favorite picture.

Donate items to a local food bank or charity together.

Finds someone ringing a bell for the Salvation Army and make a donation. (Great to use during week 3 after watching the Big Question about Christmas.)

Draw pictures of your favorite part of the story of the birth of Jesus.

Make snow angels & play in the snow together.

TIP! This page is INTENTIONALLY LEFT BLANK for those who choose to use the cut-outs from the book rather than printing. Remember, if you'd like to print the cut-outs, you can visit **www.whatsinthebible.com/everydayemmanuel** and enter the password "**advent**" to access printable versions.

1 hour +

Make Sunday School Lady's Famous Pepparkakor.*

Set-up and decorate your Christmas tree.

Go Christmas shopping together and help your kids pick out a gift for someone else.

Go Christmas caroling.

Make Christmas cookies.

Decorate Christmas cookies.

Have a special family dinner where everyone dresses up and use your nice plates/china that's usually reserved for company and holidays. You could even eat your meal by candlelight to make it extra special and let kids invite a friend.

TIP! This page is INTENTIONALLY LEFT BLANK for those who choose to use the cut-outs from the book rather than printing. Remember, if you'd like to print the cut-outs, you can visit **www.whatsinthebible.com/everydayemmanuel** and enter the password "**advent**" to access printable versions.

Have a family slumber party around the Christmas tree.

Make a special Christmas gift to give.

Watch a favorite Christmas movie together.

TIP! This page is INTENTIONALLY LEFT BLANK for those who choose to use the cut-outs from the book rather than printing. Remember, if you'd like to print the cut-outs, you can visit **www.whatsinthebible.com/everydayemmanuel** and enter the password "**advent**" to access printable versions.

WRITE YOUR OWN

TIP! Use these notes to make your own family traditions part of your calendar.

Part 5: Activities for the Countdown to Christmas Calendar

TIP! This page is INTENTIONALLY LEFT BLANK for those who choose to use the cut-outs from the book rather than printing. Remember, if you'd like to print the cut-outs, you can visit **www.whatsinthebible.com/everydayemmanuel** and enter the password "**advent**" to access printable versions.

Part 6:
PROVIDED ACTIVITIES

 TIP! You can print extra copies of these from **whatsinthebible.com/everydayemmanuel** using the password **"advent"**. You'll also find a note to use in your calendar for each activity in Part 5 – the notes with corresponding activities are starred to make them easy to find!

1. Christmas Bingo

2. What I Love About Christmas printable

3. Christmas Word Game

4. Sunday School Lady's Pepparkakor Recipe

5. Christmas Verse Cut-Outs

6. Coloring Pages

7. Christmas Cards

TIP! This page is INTENTIONALLY LEFT BLANK for those who choose to use the cut-outs from the book rather than printing. Remember, if you'd like to print the cut-outs, you can visit **www.whatsinthebible.com/everydayemmanuel** and enter the password "**advent**" to access printable versions.

CHRISTMAS BINGO

Play Christmas BINGO anytime-while you're out running errands, traveling, or even while watching Christmas movies. Cross out each image as you see it. See if you can get four in a row-BINGO!

TIP! This page is INTENTIONALLY LEFT BLANK for those who choose to use the cut-outs from the book rather than printing. Remember, if you'd like to print the cut-outs, you can visit **www.whatsinthebible.com/everydayemmanuel** and enter the password "**advent**" to access printable versions.

My favorite Christmas song is…

My favorite Christmas present is…

At Christmas-time I love to eat…

My favorite Christmas movie is…

The best part about Christmas is…

TIP! Say these out loud as a family, or write them down!

TIP! This page is INTENTIONALLY LEFT BLANK for those who choose to use the cut-outs from the book rather than printing. Remember, if you'd like to print the cut-outs, you can visit **www.whatsinthebible.com/everydayemmanuel** and enter the password "**advent**" to access printable versions.

BUCK DENVER's CHRISTMAS WORD CHALLENGE

See how many smaller words you can create using the letters from the words "Merry Christmas." For an added challenge, divide the family up into two teams and see which team can make the most words in 5 minutes.

Visit whatsinthebible.com/everydayemmanuel for the answers. We found a total of 152 possible words.

TIP! This page is INTENTIONALLY LEFT BLANK for those who choose to use the cut-outs from the book rather than printing. Remember, if you'd like to print the cut-outs, you can visit **www.whatsinthebible.com/everydayemmanuel** and enter the password "**advent**" to access printable versions.

SUNDAY SCHOOL LADY'S
PEPPARKAKOR
(SWEDISH GINGERBREAD)
RECIPE

Make your own batch of Sunday School Lady's Famous Pepparkakor using this recipe and then share it with your friends. Be sure to save one for Cap'n Pete!

INGREDIENTS

1/2 cup of unsalted butter at room temperature (1 stick)

1/3 cup brown sugar

1/4 cup white sugar

1 egg

1/4 cup of molasses or sorghum

1 tbsp maple syrup

2 cups all purpose flour

1 tsp baking soda

1/2 tsp. ground ginger

1 tsp cinnamon

1/2 tsp nutmeg

1/2 tsp cloves

1/2 tsp salt

METHOD

Cream butter and sugars with a hand or stand mixer; beat until fluffy. Add one egg; beat until thoroughly combined. Add molasses and maple syrup. Beat until combined. In a separate bowl, whisk together flour, baking soda, and spices. Add flour mix to butter mix; beat until combined. Shape dough into flat disc. Wrap in plastic wrap and refrigerate at least 4 hours (up to overnight).

WHEN READY TO BAKE

Preheat oven to 325 and lightly grease 2 baking sheets. Roll out dough thinly and cut cookies out using cookie cutters. Place on baking sheets. Bake 8-10 minutes.

TIP! Cut them out in the shape of a star to make them look like Sunday School Lady's!

TIP! This page is INTENTIONALLY LEFT BLANK for those who choose to use the cut-outs from the book rather than printing. Remember, if you'd like to print the cut-outs, you can visit **www.whatsinthebible.com/everydayemmanuel** and enter the password "**advent**" to access printable versions.

THE TRUE MEANING OF CHRISTMAS

Cut out and use these cards to help your family learn the real reason we celebrate Christmas.

For to us a child is born, to us a son is given; and the government shall be upon his shoulder, and his name shall be called Wonderful Counselor, Mighty God, Everlasting Father, Prince of Peace.

ISAIAH 9:6

For to us a child is born, to us a son is given; and the government shall be upon his shoulder, and his name shall be called Wonderful Counselor, Mighty God, Everlasting Father, Prince of Peace.

ISAIAH 9:6

For to us a child is born, to us a son is given; and the government shall be upon his shoulder, and his name shall be called Wonderful Counselor, Mighty God, Everlasting Father, Prince of Peace.

ISAIAH 9:6

For to us a child is born, to us a son is given; and the government shall be upon his shoulder, and his name shall be called Wonderful Counselor, Mighty God, Everlasting Father, Prince of Peace.

ISAIAH 9:6

For to us a child is born, to us a son is given; and the government shall be upon his shoulder, and his name shall be called Wonderful Counselor, Mighty God, Everlasting Father, Prince of Peace.

ISAIAH 9:6

For to us a child is born, to us a son is given; and the government shall be upon his shoulder, and his name shall be called Wonderful Counselor, Mighty God, Everlasting Father, Prince of Peace.

ISAIAH 9:6

TIP! This page is INTENTIONALLY LEFT BLANK for those who choose to use the cut-outs from the book rather than printing. Remember, if you'd like to print the cut-outs, you can visit **www.whatsinthebible.com/everydayemmanuel** and enter the password "**advent**" to access printable versions.

THE TRUE MEANING OF CHRISTMAS

Cut out and use these cards to help your family learn the real reason we celebrate Christmas.

For unto you is born this day in the city of David a Savior, who is Christ the Lord.
LUKE 2:11

For unto you is born this day in the city of David a Savior, who is Christ the Lord.
LUKE 2:11

For unto you is born this day in the city of David a Savior, who is Christ the Lord.
LUKE 2:11

For unto you is born this day in the city of David a Savior, who is Christ the Lord.
LUKE 2:11

For unto you is born this day in the city of David a Savior, who is Christ the Lord.
LUKE 2:11

For unto you is born this day in the city of David a Savior, who is Christ the Lord.
LUKE 2:11

TIP! This page is INTENTIONALLY LEFT BLANK for those who choose to use the cut-outs from the book rather than printing. Remember, if you'd like to print the cut-outs, you can visit **www.whatsinthebible.com/everydayemmanuel** and enter the password "**advent**" to access printable versions.

"For to us a child is born, to us a son is given..." ISAIAH 9:6

TIP! This page is INTENTIONALLY LEFT BLANK for those who choose to use the cut-outs from the book rather than printing. Remember, if you'd like to print the cut-outs, you can visit **www.whatsinthebible.com/everydayemmanuel** and enter the password "**advent**" to access printable versions.

TIP! This page is INTENTIONALLY LEFT BLANK for those who choose to use the cut-outs from the book rather than printing. Remember, if you'd like to print the cut-outs, you can visit **www.whatsinthebible.com/everydayemmanuel** and enter the password "**advent**" to access printable versions.

TIP! This page is INTENTIONALLY LEFT BLANK for those who choose to use the cut-outs from the book rather than printing. Remember, if you'd like to print the cut-outs, you can visit **www.whatsinthebible.com/everydayemmanuel** and enter the password **"advent"** to access printable versions.

TIP! This page is INTENTIONALLY LEFT BLANK for those who choose to use the cut-outs from the book rather than printing. Remember, if you'd like to print the cut-outs, you can visit **www.whatsinthebible.com/everydayemmanuel** and enter the password "**advent**" to access printable versions.

WISHING YOU A VERY MERRY CHRISTMAS

www.WhatsInTheBible.com

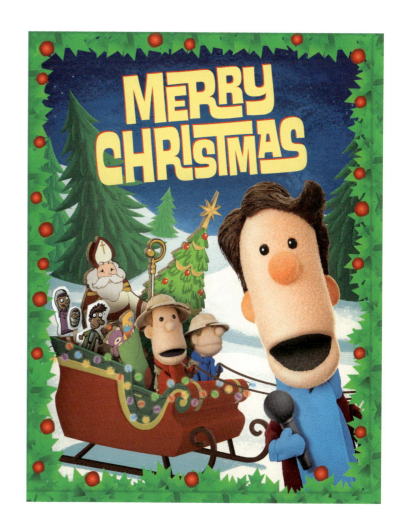

TIP! This page is INTENTIONALLY LEFT BLANK for those who choose to use the cut-outs from the book rather than printing. Remember, if you'd like to print the cut-outs, you can visit **www.whatsinthebible.com/everydayemmanuel** and enter the password "**advent**" to access printable versions.

MERRY CHRISTMAS (upside down)

EVERYDAY EMMANUEL

www.WhatsInTheBible.com

TIP! This page is INTENTIONALLY LEFT BLANK for those who choose to use the cut-outs from the book rather than printing. Remember, if you'd like to print the cut-outs, you can visit **www.whatsinthebible.com/everydayemmanuel** and enter the password "**advent**" to access printable versions.

TIP! This page is INTENTIONALLY LEFT BLANK for those who choose to use the cut-outs from the book rather than printing. Remember, if you'd like to print the cut-outs, you can visit **www.whatsinthebible.com/everydayemmanuel** and enter the password "**advent**" to access printable versions.